You don't have to be a scuba diver to plunge into the wonderful world of undersea life. Now you can fold and cut out rows of marvelous sea creatures from the mighty whale and the graceful flying fish to the wriggly Moray eel and the smallest starfish. Just follow the simple instructions below, folding the special colored paper provided or making your own. It's a great way to explore the strange and exciting secrets of the deep.

How to make the chains

1 Remove the templates and the printed papers by carefully lifting the staples in the middle of the book. Then press the staples flat.

2 Choose a printed paper. Fold it in half, and then fold the top and bottom edges back to meet the central fold. This makes the accordion fold you need to have for a paper chain of four linked shapes. For a pair of shapes, use a piece of paper half the size and simply fold it in half. For a single shape, there's no need to fold the paper. If you are using your own paper, see page 2.

3 Position your template on the folded paper, following any special instructions printed on the template. You will notice that the template slightly overlaps the paper on both sides. These are the edges that you must leave uncut. They keep the shapes connected to make a chain.

4 Hold the template firmly with your spare hand, and then trace a line carefully around the inside of the shape, keeping your pencil next to the edge.

5 Cut out the shape, holding the folded paper firmly and cutting through all the layers at once. REMEMBER NOT TO CUT ALONG THE FOLD LINES. Now open up the folds to reveal your paper chain ... and watch out for a sinister school of sharks.

These ocean-life templates have been designed to fit sheets of paper 11 inches high by at least 7½ inches wide (28 x 19cm) folded into four. Use the printed paper provided, and make your own as well – just fold and cut any paper as long as it is not too thick. You will find lots of hints for coloring below and on pages 3–4. The most important thing to remember is that accurate folding is essential, no matter what paper you use.

Coloring the chains

Decorating paper is lots of fun. You can use crayons or markers on white or colored backgrounds before or after you make your chains. Try adding glitter or metallic color to imitate fish scales.

You can also use the templates as stencils to make gift wrap (for stenciling instructions see page 31).

IMPORTANT NOTE

Remember that if you use your own paper, it must be exactly 11 inches (28cm) high, so trim it to size if necessary. The width of the paper must be at least 7½ inches (19cm). If you want a longer chain, it is better to make several paper chains and join them together, rather than trying to cut accurately through a thick sheet of folded paper.

TROPICAL REEF FISH

Coral reefs are home to hundreds of different fish, attracted by the rich food supply or protection they offer. Their brilliant color and patterns make good camouflage.

Use your brightest colors and let your imagination run wild.

SCALLOP AND STARFISH

Scallops and starfish are seafloor animals. Starfish can live at any depth – even in the deepest ocean – but scallops live only in the shallows.

Color the scallop pale pink and brown; if you darken the grooves the ridges will stand out. Starfish are bright orange with rows of red or blue dots.

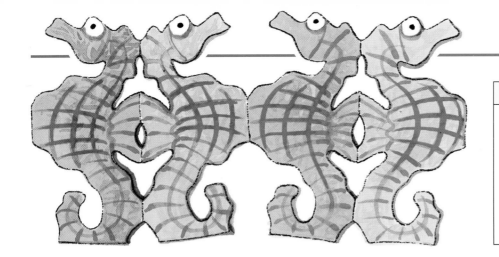

SEA HORSE

No more than 1 foot (30cm) tall, sea horses move about in an upright position and use their tails to grip seaweed. Males protect the eggs in a pouch until they hatch.

Make them gray or brown with darker stripes, or go wild with zany colors.

DOLPHIN

Probably the most intelligent of all sea creatures, dolphins are mammals, not fish, and cannot breathe underwater. They are members of the toothed-whale family.

Use dark gray and blue for tail and flippers. Add friendly eyes and a "smile."

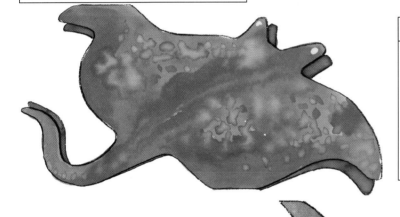

MANTA RAY

Most rayfish live on the ocean bed, but manta rays live at the surface, where they feed by skimming along, scooping up small sea creatures. "Wingspan" can be 19 feet (6m).

Color them light brown and then add spots and patches of darker brown.

SHARK

With no covers over their gills, sharks have to keep swimming or drown! They have skeletons made of cartilage instead of bone, and rows of very sharp teeth.

Sharks are gray, blue, or brown. Some are spotted and striped.

SQUID

Squid move by siphoning up water, and expelling it to shoot backward or forward at speed. If threatened, they spray black ink and disappear.

For realism use white paper and make the edges blue, yellow, and pink – but fantasy colors are much more fun.

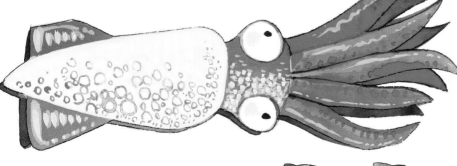

FLYING FISH

These have large fins that can be spread out to make wings. When hunted by other fish, they leap out of the water and glide above the surface for almost 60 seconds.

Color them gray, green, and blue, and add highlights of pink and glitter.

WHALE

There are many different types of whale. All are air-breathing mammals. Some can stay under-water for 2 hours, and the fastest can travel up to 46mph (74km/h).

Color your whale brown or in a blend of blue and black with a paler belly.

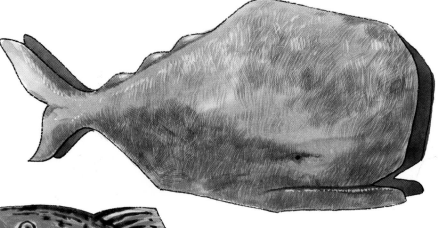

SALMON

Salmon begin life in rivers, then swim down to the sea, traveling up to 1500 miles (2400km) from their hatching places. They return to breed, and the cycle begins again.

Color them turquoise, green, and gray, with a streak of glitter.

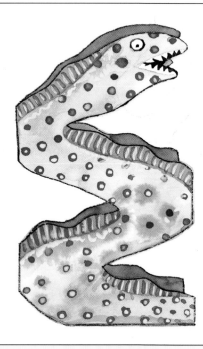

SEA TURTLE

These air-breathing reptiles, who return to land to lay their eggs, are not adult for 20 years, and live for up to 75 years. Some live on sea grass, while others eat fish.

Draw the shell pattern lightly in pencil first; then color with shades of green, yellow, or brown.

MORAY EEL

This large eel with razor-sharp teeth makes its home in rock crevices, hiding its long body while it waits for its prey. It strikes by pushing against a rock to propel itself forward.

For realism, use purple and brown criss crosses – or go wild with magic markers as we have done.

Now that you know how to make and decorate paper chains, put your new skill to use with this exciting collection of creative ideas. If you have used up all the printed papers, design your own – page 2 tells you how. Why not use bright neon crayons, markers, and some glitter to add that extra zing? You'll need your BASICS BOX for all these projects – see inside front cover.

THE WHALE CARD

It only takes minutes to turn a sheet of paper into this very special card, and you can have fun thinking up messages to go inside. How about, "I'm having a BIG pool party" or "Thanks, I had a whale of a time!?"

You will need

BASICS BOX; ½ whale paper chain (2 linked shapes) – *use light card stock (see pages 1 and 2 for instructions)*; 1 piece blue paper – *3½ x 3½ inches (9 x 9cm)*; 1 envelope – *measure the card and add ½ inch (1cm) all around*

How to make

Fold your paper chain in half to make a card. Use your markers to decorate it, and don't forget to add a smile.

Roll up the blue paper, and secure one end with tape. Snip down toward the tape about five times. Separate the cut ends, curling them round a pencil. Cut a small hole in the whale's head, and insert the "spout," securing it inside with small pieces of tape.

THE DOLPHIN POP-UP CARD

You will need

BASICS BOX; colored card stock (blue or turquoise) – *1 piece 8 x 10 inches (20 x 25cm) folded in half, for the card*; ½ dolphin paper chain (2 linked shapes) – *use light card stock (see pages 1 and 2 for instructions)*; 1 envelope – *measure card and add ½ inch (1cm) all around*

How to make

Open the card and position the dolphin shapes over the fold as shown. Your aim is to fix their tail fins an equal distance from the fold. Use a pencil to mark their positions, judging the distance by eye or measuring it. Color and decorate your dolphins and the inside of the card. Attach the dolphins' tails to the card with small pieces of tape as shown. The dolphins will now leap into the air every time you open the card. Write your message inside.

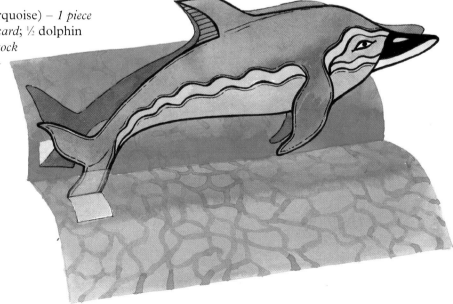

MAGNETIC FISHING GAME
(for 2 or more players)

You will need
BASICS BOX; light card stock – *for a selection of sea creatures*; paper clips; sticks – *at least 10 inches (25cm) long*; string; small magnets; 1 grocery carton; craft knife; blue paper or blue poster paint – *to decorate the carton*

How to make
Use the templates and card stock to make as many single shapes as you like (see page 1). Decorate each sea creature and mark it with a different number. Attach a paper clip to each of them. Make the rods by tying a length of string to one end of each stick and then tying a magnet to the other end of the string. Ask an adult to help you cut off the flaps which form the lid of the carton. Line the inside with paper, or paint it blue. Decorate the outside too.

How to play
Place the sea creatures inside the carton. Take turns dangling your rods into it without looking. When you catch a fish, write down its number. This is your score for the round. When all of them have been caught, the winner is the fisher who has scored most points.

STARFISH FRAME

You will need
BASICS BOX; 1 sheet of corrugated card stock and 2 sheets of plain card stock – *14½ x 11 inches (37 x 28cm)*; double-sided tape; poster paint; 4 starfish paper chains – *see pages 1 and 2 for instructions*

How to make
To create the frame, measure and mark a 3¼ inch (8cm) border round the corrugated card stock. Ask an adult to cut out the central section. Stick the corrugated card stock and one of the plain card sheets together by using lengths of double-sided tape along three sides – leave one short side open.

To create a support, fold the other plain sheet in half. Cut a wedge shape from the bottom half as shown. Then stick the top half to the back of the frame. Bend the wedge backward until the frame stands up.

Paint the front of the frame, and leave to dry. Snip a starfish from two chains to make two chains of 4 starfish and two of 3. Decorate and glue into position. Slide a picture or collage of photos into the frame.

STENCILED T-SHIRT
You can use the ocean templates as stencils to print your very own T-shirt designs. It is so easy – just follow our instructions, and read the guidelines on your fabric paints to make the design permanent.

You will need
BASICS BOX; T-shirt – *plain color, washed and ironed*; starfish and sea horse templates; masking tape – *to secure stencil*; fabric paint – *any color*; fabric pens or small, stiff-bristled paint brush; iron – *for sealing the design, if necessary (see below)*

How to make
Cover your work surface with newspaper. Fold more newspaper to make a large, smooth backing pad, and place it inside the T-shirt. Smooth the fabric until it lies flat. Use masking tape to secure the sea horse template in position. Hold it firmly with your spare hand and dab the paint onto the fabric, working from the edges inward. If using a brush, do not overload it, or the paint will spread under the stencil. Leave the stencil and newspaper in place until the paint is dry. Repeat the process to stencil a starfish on each side. Follow the instructions on your fabric paint about sealing the design, and ask an adult to help you do this.

DESK CADDY
Paint an empty can a good background color, using acrylic enamel paint, and leave it to dry. Glue a decorated paper chain around the can. Protect it with acrylic varnish, and glue a circle of felt to the base to protect your desk, if you like.

BOOK AND FOLDER COVERS
You'll never have trouble locating your books again if you decorate them with ocean paper chains. Choose strong background colors and your brightest markers. Just glue the chains in rows on the front cover or fold them round the book or folder to cover the front and back. For a longer-lasting finish, you could add self-adhesive laminating film.

OCEANARIUM

Make a window on the deep sea world with a model of life on the seabed.

You will need

BASICS BOX; 1 rectangular carton – *for aquarium*; craft knife; poster paints – *yellow, pink, blue, and green*; construction paper – *for sea anemones and seaweed*; thin card stock – *for sea creatures*; pebbles; sand; needle and thread; reusable adhesive

How to make

Ask an adult to help you prepare the carton – you need to remove three of the lid flaps and trim the fourth to make the front edge as shown in the diagram. Paint the inside of the carton. Use yellow for the seabed and blue and green for the sides and top, mixing them for a good undersea color. Secure the flap inside with tape.

Make some sea anemones, following the instructions for the whale's spout on page 29, but using squares 2½ x 2½ inches (6.5 x 6.5cm) colored pink or yellow.

Cut out some seaweed shapes with wide "trunks" and lots of wiggly branches (see diagram). Color them green and glue them to the sides of the carton. Arrange the sand and pebbles on the seabed.

Use the templates to make as many single sea creatures as you wish (see page 1). Then decorate them in any colors you choose.

Ask an adult to help you position the swimming creatures. Use a needle to attach a knotted thread to each of them, then push the needle and thread up through the top of the carton, and secure it on the outside with tape.

Arrange the anemones and starfish on the seabed, using reusable adhesive to keep them in place.

Seaweed

Sea anemone